D1297176

Letters from The Gardeners Cottage

The first full year of rewilding a life on the west coast of Scotland.

SL SOURWINE

www.SLSourwine.com

Gratefully dedicated to my
Patreon subscribers
who delighted me by wanting
the letters in the first place.

CONTENTS

How to Get A Letter

Introduction

In late March of 2019 I was fantasy scrolling properties to buy in Scotland (that I couldn't afford) when all of a sudden I decided to hit the "To Let" (rent) tab on the website. I wasn't looking in Argyll. I had never been to this part of Scotland even, so I don't remember how I managed a search that would turn up this place. But there it was, a three bedroom cottage with a greenhouse set against a walled garden on a large estate. I realised it just might be possible to start actually living the life I was dreaming about much sooner. I had been putting that life off because of the narrow way I thought I could accomplish it.

So I booked a viewing.

I didn't even have the money to come see The Gardeners Cottage at the time, let alone to pay deposits and move here. My wonderful neighbour Bridget somehow understood the urgency and hunger that was in me at the time. It wasn't very sensible! She gave me gas money. So I loaded up my dog Alfred, packed a cooler full of food and camping kit to make the car warm enough to sleep in and a stove to make coffee and dinner. I drove 10 hours from the south coast of England to the edges of Loch Striven on the Cowal peninsula and found a place to sleep before my appointment the next day.

When I arrived at The Cottage I knew I wanted to be here very badly. There was competition as the listing had received a lot of interest. As I was taking a walk around the grounds before leaving I had my first conversation with the land here. I told it I would very much like to be here and if it wanted me to be part of its story perhaps it could see to it that I got chosen. And I did.

It's not the first time in my life that I answered a strong call that didn't make much sense to anyone but me. In 2009 I had left my wonderful job as a

Vice President in a good company in Seattle and emigrated to the UK without a job or even much money. It turned out wonderfully. Before that I had left my native Canada for the job in Seattle. So I understood re-birthing and change quite a bit. This time I was really at a cross-roads. I knew I had to change a lot about my life if I wanted to have any shot at putting the best of myself into the world. I wanted to write and create things, use my hands, reignite my passion for nature, and feel like I was contributing to our global environment in a positive way.

One of the hard truths I had to face about why I wasn't doing any of that was because I was exhausted and not a little battle-scarred from my career. My identity had been very tied to my work, and I was good at it and well paid for it, the trouble was it had started to make me miserable. I was no longer able or willing to fight the fights required to be a female senior executive in this world. And a couple of bruising reminders of what was required to keep going on that path had really impacted me. It was hard to understand how something I had completely loved for so long became painful for me. I even tried to reignite it with a new creative project about it because that was all I knew. But it didn't work. At the time I discovered The Cottage I had just fired my last consulting client, left myself without an ongoing income, and knew I needed to make a different life now.

So I leapt. And in April 2019 I moved moved to Scotland to stay.

I decided to create the Letters from the Gardeners Cottage to capture the experience of changing my life and to make a commitment to my creativity that I wouldn't break! I wanted to inspire and connect with others that were feeling this deeper hunger too. And I thought of the Letters as a way to share what I consider my very good fortune to be in this space. The first letter went out in May 2019 to about ten subscribers including my Mom. As I write this in early 2021 I am closing in on 1,000 letters sent! Isn't that a miraculous thing? The collection of letters in this book are the first twelve. I hope reading them brings you joy and restfulness. May you notice and nurture the wild in yourself and the living whole of which you are a part.

MAY 2019

The Gardeners Cottage
Argyll's Secret Coast
Scotland, UK

May 20, 2019

Dear friends,

I'm sitting at the window (my computer is currently placed in a deep window sash and I am in one of the armchairs as a seat as my new desk doesn't arrive until Tuesday) and wanting to begin our first letter together, but I am constantly distracted by the goings on on the other side of the glass. There seems to be a territory dispute amongst a few butterflies. I'm not sure where the line is, but it is definitely being crossed repeatedly and everyone is quite aflutter about the situation. Some birds which I have yet to determine are swallows or swifts are doing a fly-by between the tree across the drive and the centre of my window. It's quite wonderful and totally steals your eyes from the page.

I can't thank you enough for becoming my very first Patrons and wanting to receive these monthly missives from me and all the plants and creatures here at The Gardeners Cottage. It's such a privilege to be here and then to get to share it this way too, well to say it fills my heart with joy is an understatement. Thank you.

This little book published over a century ago in 1910 although very wrong about where honey comes from, nevertheless has delightful illustrations and descriptions of so many of the flowers I find. It's a treat to use it instead of just Google.

Being here at the cottage, even for the short time I've managed so far, is really bringing me back in tune with the cycles of nature. The way the first warmth of spring brings the joyful eruption of daffodils and cheerful wild primroses rise out of the darkness of mud and last year's leaves. Then, if you are lucky, the magic blue carpet of bluebells paints the forest floor. To those of us not raised on these particular islands how mythical that is to our eyes to see. I used to drive as far away as was necessary to get the thrill of that sight. I have found here in this little fairy-tale cottage of mine that I am completely surrounded by them. The abundance of it all is a little embarrassing.

This first month of transition I am reminded of the cycles of my own life too. How despite the formality of school and work timetables that we too have natural cycles of bloom and retreat, growth, and rest. That things need to finish sometimes so the next thing can come. That some things like the sturdy ancient oaks and scotch pine are less changeable and hold the scene for some of the seasonal shows. It makes me think about this move and placing of myself here in this place has been part of a return cycle for me. A return to a more intimate relationship with nature whose importance to me was one of the first true things I knew about myself. I am also being reminded again and again to go a bit slower to forget my PhD in the School of Get It All Done at Once! I am excited to settle more into the myths and magic of this place too and share some stories that connect those things to my experience here.

The Cottage from the exterior of the walled garden.

The furnishing of the house is an on-going process. I'm trying really hard to do as much as I can in a zero-waste/ recycle/reuse way. I've been shopping in charity shops and using Facebook marketplace to get some amazing free pieces. My friends have contributed their own unused or excess goods including a television and a Nespresso machine to the effort! There have been some stunning finds like my 120 year-old Athol Royal Dalton china set, the beautiful William Morris patterned sofa, the free tools for the fire place, a free kitchen garbage bin (wish there were more of those!), paintings, bookcases, and chairs. It will be so wonderful to keep adding to the house in a thoughtful manner.

I did order myself a bed, desk and mattress this week to be delivered. I have over a month here uninterrupted on this stretch and I realised that if I was to settle down and get to work and not be on permanent vacation I needed to sleep properly and to have a place to work. The curation of things is much easier down in the south where all the people are, so I allow myself the permission to be imperfect while I try. As one of my favourite accounts on Instagram @zerowastechef says: we don't need a few people doing zero waste perfectly, we need millions doing it imperfectly.

Weeds! Well, not just weeds, but they are the general theme of all my gardening efforts at the moment. I have decided that just a bit of effort each day will eventually make a huge difference. On sunny days I work out in the gardens, on rainy days I will work in the greenhouse. We'll see if I get enough of both. May has been splendid up here. Very sunny and very dry. Not all you are used to

My work ahead of me in the untended walled garden.

hearing about Scotland! I'm sure I'll wash away an entire month at some point with rain and your letter will be filled with a description of all the different kinds of raindrops! But for now it has been glorious.

There are so many beautiful plants that are trying to make themselves known despite being choked by weeds and grass at the moment. One of the most delightful finds has been all the wild strawberry plants that have managed to hide here and there around the garden and rocks. Cannot wait to taste the sunshine in them with my breakfast! But that's usually for June.

There are so many plants I do not know the name of, or what they will become, only tall stalks of last year's flowering to indicate "watch this space." So I am gently going around and introducing myself as I can. At the moment there are peonies—pink and yellow. A soft pink clematis that marks my gate into the walled garden. There is a lonely iris who has managed to push her way through the scrub grass to flower all by herself. I have found out that the other type of fruit tree in the greenhouse is an apricot! One of my favourites. The tree is so heavy with fruit, hopefully we'll see it ripen this summer along with the peaches and grapes. There are chives which have had a party all over the garden while no one was watching. Thyme grows in the rock wall at the base of the greenhouse. And I have discovered some asparagus outside the guest room door! It will be so much abundance here. So much to come.

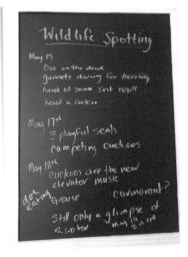

I'm trying to keep track of all the wonder I'm seeing!

All The Wonderful Creatures

The animals about the estate have been my favourite part. Each day I keep track of what I have seen or heard so that I can remember what happened. And so I can remember to go look up everything that is new to me! I'll try and write more about them all in our letters.

There is a little doe who likes to eat the trees in my front garden and comes by most days.

Everyday I go to check in and see if I will be so lucky as to spot some seals (maybe my favourite part of the day). So far

I have encountered over 20! Twelve at once, otherwise but I don't know how many of are return visitors. Maybe I'll get to know them eventually!

The little bird I painted on your envelope is called a Great Tit. It was the first bird call I heard when I moved here. If you go on the internet and search "Great Tit Bird song" you'll find a lot of YouTube videos that feature its special sound. It's described as like a "squeaky door" because of the even rhythm of it. If you go listen you'll have a wonderful idea of what it sounds like to be in the garden here.

Here are a couple of the more exotic creatures I've run into:

The Slow Worm.

The UK's only legless lizard! It is a protected species here in the UK and I'm so pleased to find them present here on the estate. The can grow up to 50cm (about 20 inches) long and can live for up to 20 years!!! This one was sunning on one of the first warm days along the footpath through the grassland on the way to the sea.

The Rove Beetle.

I'll talk about a couple of species that are found here on the estate each month. I hope that's as fun for you as it is for me! There are lots I haven't even been able to figure out exactly what they are and am trying to get a good enough picture on one of my walks to get some help.

"In every walk with nature one receives
far more than he seeks."
~ *John Muir*

Much love,
Susie x

The Gardeners Cottage
Argyll's Secret Coast
Scotland, UK

June 14, 2019

Greetings from wild and beautiful Argyll.

Today as I write the action outside my window is mostly wind jostled plants trying to

The table where I sit most mornings watching for seals. Imagine yourself here with me if you like!

hold on to their petals like holding down a flowy skirt on a breezy day at the seaside! The roses appeared to be quite tough, but the clematis over the entrance to the walled garden I fear succumbed to the last bout of wind. The protection of the walled garden is so important here for the more fragile things.

Speaking of fragile things I wanted to write to you a little bit about the harder parts of the experience of this much change. Even the best stuff which is actioning a dream into place. I know it doesn't look like it from the outside if you've known me for a while, but I find it so hard reaching for my dreams. I know I've made big decisions before like quitting my job in Seattle and moving to the UK. I managed to eventually take action, but it isn't a fast or pretty process.

As I try to bring something important to me into being I do a whole bunch of freezing up, becoming really slow to act on easy things, a little self sabotage, a lot of self doubt, and always always answering an internal question of whether I'm worthy of it. It's not something anyone else will ever be able to tell me and each time I have to struggle it out with whatever part of myself still worries about that. Sometimes it happens fast, and sometimes it takes a while. I now, mostly, recognise what's happening and can activate some of the things that I've learned after all these years to help myself along.

I use self care—rest being one of the most important for me. If I force myself everything gets much worse. I try to consistently doubt the part of me that doubts my worth. Do I really believe the thoughts and fears that part of my mind is serving up in response to the discomfort of the new? I do the things I can in the moment. Can I send that one email? Move that one thing? Make that one call, etc that's enough. And I also try

The male Dark Green Fritillary butterfly, the green is on the underside of his wings.

to specifically notice and share the things I love, the beautiful things I see or do–it's why I love Instagram so much! When I've managed to pile enough of the good against the doubt, things shift and I can get back at taking the action I need to keep reaching for my dream. I've learned that this is a cycle of mine and try not to find myself too wrong while it's happening. Things like moving to a cottage in Scotland definitely spark it! The first few weeks living here were full of slamming on the brakes and finding action hard to take. It's mostly shifted now, but I just wanted to share this in case you feel like this sometimes and it stops you for longer. You're not alone.

About the house

The work about the house had been mostly been me versus the spiders. Spiders are amazing and they eat so many other bugs. My intent in the last month has been to block up their food supply enough that I no longer required their services! This old house hasn't had much care for a while and so I spent most of the month tackling corners and closets to fill in holes around pipes and windows and in the woodwork that will put an end to the house being the main freeway between the front garden and the walled garden. I've also managed to patch up and paint the inside of the guest suite's private door. I figure I will move my way around the house from the guest quarters outwards with my large can of putty and my spatula. I will always be Chief of Spider Incidents though for anyone who happens to come and stay.

The most exciting thing for me was the arrival of my fridge-freezer I have lived with a small under counter fridge with basically an ice cube compartment freezer for the last decade. That is not how you get on well, at least somewhere this remote, and I'm now completely ready to stock up and have space to process some of the fresh and wonderful things I'll be growing and forging too. My lovely neighbours at Dovecote Cottage have their beer fridge back after kindly showing up with it at my door for me to use for the last two weeks! Neighbours are the best. This week the other closest neighbours at Swallows Nest brought down a bag of seed potatoes! I hope to be in charge of distributing apricots and peaches from the greenhouse. Fingers crossed!

I feel embarrassed about something since I moved here. I'm embarrassed about how much I didn't know or notice the names of things. There are thousands of different plants and animals around me here. So many of them completely unknown to me. I might have seen them before, but I couldn't name them or tell you their story, or their uses, or the role they play in our landscape. I've always been a lover of nature, but I was I wasn't paying attention.

A female stag beetle with quite a story to tell! It can take up to six years for one beetle to emerge as an adult. Six years!

Being here and having the time and purpose to look closely has changed everything. I'm embarrassed that I didn't do better before, even when it was just walking down the street. No wonder our natural world is in crisis. So one of the ways I'm rewilding myself on this journey is committing to learn the names and stories of at least 100 new things this year. Plants, animals, insects. I'll share some of them with you as I go along.

The bird sound that dominated this month was the cuckoo. I haven't seen one yet but they are every where here and as I'm walking or gardening I hear them as clearly as my grandfather Gabriel's clock striking the hour. It makes me think of him every time, and that's a really nice surprise.

The bird who wanted the most attention and made me learn his name is an adorable fellow called the Pied Wagtail. Its official description, and image, from the Royal Society for the Protection of Birds calls it "a delightful small, long-tailed and rather sprightly black and white bird. When not standing and frantically wagging its tail up and down it can be seen dashing over lawns or car parks in search of food." The wagtail part is so true! I adore them and though they are widespread across the UK this is our first official meeting.

Each morning I still go to call on the seals. It's been a few days since I've caught any and I miss them! One of the little deer has jumped the garden gate and had a couple nights sleep in the walled garden. The flattened plants make a nice cosy nest! If she ate weeds I'd leave the gate wide open for her.

My roe deer visitor outside my desk window.

She's a Roe Deer and last night when we went for a walk and we surprised her, she barked her alarm so loudly. I'd never heard a deer make that noise before. She did it a few times in row or I might not have believed my ears. If you want to hear it look up 'roe deer barking' it's really something!

There are a group of goslings emerged on the pond out with the Highland Cattle and the swallows, which have nested under my eaves, have a bunch of hungry little mouths peeking over the edge of the nest.

All the Pretty Flowers

Everything is happening so fast now that we are well into June and weeds. Definitely the weeds are thriving. Every day when I go on my rounds I try to take at least a handful of weeds and grass out of the walled garden beds. I see so many new faces. Lots here still to be discovered. It's the wildflowers that have really stole the show for the most part though. The flower I painted on your envelopes this month is the Foxglove.

Fairy handprints in the Foxglove flower.

They're beautiful and bright pink with speckled insides. In Scottish Gaelic (I learned this month that you pronounce Scottish Gaelic like Gal-lic and Irish as Gay-lic) the flower is called lus nam ban-sith 'the fairy woman's plant.'

As the markings on the flower were thought to be the hand prints of fairies. Foxglove is also actual medicine for the heart. It was the original source of the ingredient for the modern heart medication dioxin. But dosage is important and it is poisonous when consumed directly! Foxglove is also the official County flower of Argyll and so fitting that I chose to paint it. This morning on my walk I encountered one of the flowers that grew as tall as my nose! Wonderful.

The coast, fields, and burns (streams) are also taken over with glorious yellow irises. Every edge has a grouping of their cheerful faces. There are thousands of them around here and it makes for stunning scenes. I've yet to be able to take a picture that captures its impact correctly.

In the walled garden there are snapdragons growing up the walls—I didn't know they would do that! And so many other plants are looking to burst open and reveal what they are. The wild strawberries give me one or two to taste everyday now. I've got a good start on planting some food and herbs in the greenhouse to get me through the year before we have a proper garden next summer. I've grown my first things from seed (peas) and I'm very proud of myself.

A beautiful purple poppy found its way into the gravel on the greenhouse floor and has provided me with two stunning blooms. I hope to manage to collect the seeds and successfully transplant it out into one of the garden beds once the second bloom is finished.

I'm so lucky in the abundance of beauty that wraps itself around this place. And I'm so willing to share! I'm ready to take official reservations for those seeking retreat into this little bit of the planet. I'll post more of the detail on the Patreon site if you're interested. It would really be a home stay experience all your needs will be met for your stay and you can meld into the rhythm the days here as much or as little as you like. My first "test" guest is one of my favourite painters and a friend from the south of England. She's coming to stay to do some sketching and shake up her normal practise while getting a good rest and just surrounding herself with nature. I can't wait.

But until I can welcome you in person I want to thank you again for letting me write to you of my experience here. There's so much to tell you I've started a list so that I don't leave anything out. Until next month.

"What if we turn the old nursery rhymes and fairy tales we all know into feral creatures once again, set them loose in new lands to root through the acorn fall of oak trees? What else is there to do if we want to keep any of the wildness of the world, and of ourselves?"
- Sylvia Linsteadt, Turning Our Fairy Tales Feral Again

Much love,
Susie xx

Flag iris along the beach.

JULY 2019

The Gardeners Cottage
Argyll's Secret Coast
Scotland, UK

July 16, 2019

Greetings from high summer at The Gardeners Cottage!

The fact that it is well and truly summer came home to me the other day when walking past the fields giving off that tall, hot, dry grass smell that only comes with sunshine and dryness. And the summer insect sounds that

The heather I've included in your envelopes as I picked it. I thought you'd like to see so you can imagine how beautiful it is here in its purpleness by the colours of Loch Fyne.

accompany the smell like the hum of grasshoppers. The bracken is taller than me in so many places and even Alfred has given up running through it because he can't bounce high enough to see where he's going. It's quite something to watch him try though.

Bracken is a growth of wild fern that unrolls itself in the Fibonacci spiral in the late spring of each year. It opens above the finishing bluebells and fills the forest floor creating deep invisible and protected spaces for the little creatures. Big ones too. This morning as I was walking home from the beach I surprised a doe who was having a lovely nap in the thickness of it just a couple of feet off the road and she vanished with only a glimpse of her lovely red coat. The bracken expands into all the spaces and totally changes your view and perspective on the landscape. But then come fall it all dies off and breaks back down and leaves the trails and sight lines visible again. It's a remarkable thing to get to stay in one place and watch the whole process.

Since I wrote you last it's been a busy month. I had another trip down south for a long planned visit with some friends from Seattle and to pick up another load of furniture and things for the house. I mostly wanted books! I've managed to get about half my books here to the cottage. I love having them with me, but I brought all the important ones for here like my guides to trees and birds of these islands. Next month I think will be tree identification month! They deserve their names.

I've also had a bit of sad news here on the estate. My lovely neighbours, a family of five who have been kind and fun and just a delight to live close to out in the middle of nowhere, are leaving next week. There were some shenanigans with the estate managers and their experience with living here was not going as promised. I'll be so sad to see them go. We have one last Friday to have our self-titled Ardmarnoch Pub Garden meet up—basically where we sit on their lawn having a beer or two while the children and dogs run around like demons. It has been a joyful part of my settling in here. Being a renter sure comes with some compromises. Wherever you go there will always be humans to deal with! Being my age though brings a lot of clarity about what you want, disinterest in drama, and better practise at laying down boundaries. Thinking about it this morning on my walk I realised regardless that what I am learning for sure is that this is the life I want. This immersion in nature. A greenhouse!! Places to walk and swim and welcome others. It's not just an idea I had anymore. I'm really clear on knowing that now and that's a gift in and of itself.

About the House

The Cottage had its first paying guest this month! Although the guest room is not complete by any means aesthetically, it's really comfortable and received a lovely review. My intention for the use of this place for guests is restfulness, being cared for, and enjoying the nature. My guest, Sally, is a brilliant painter and enjoyed her experimentation with water colours on the Scottish landscape. This was one of her sketches which she so kindly left for me. It's the view from the beach where we went wild swimming together. The official name is Ardmarnoch Bay. I love it and hopefully the printing will do it justice.

I've done more math about what it takes to actually feed and house someone and the cost of trips to the airport etc. I didn't get much work done besides all the cooking and washing up! But I'll factor that in for the future. If you or someone you know is looking for a place of deep rest and quiet please reach out. One of my motivations for taking this space was sharing it that way and I also learned I enjoyed it!

In the Greenhouse

Apricots!!! Apricots every where. More apricots than you can dream of and all coming ripe within a week of each other! So far I've given all the neighbours a bag, made two sets of jam, one set of chilli apricot chutney, and am currently in the middle of my first attempt to dry them in the oven. And there is still one flat left of them. Please send jars! LOL It's truly wonderful to see so much come off one slightly wild tree. My job for this winter will be to prune it sensitively to attempt to bring it back into a bit of control, but to also maintain its ability to fruit. Apricot only fruits on second year growth so I assume there will be a lot fo standing there staring at branches with pruners in my hand trying to figure it all out.

The peaches have come on surprisingly well and should be next to be picked, but even though there are two trees there won't even be a quarter of the apricot harvest. So guests arriving at that time can just call themselves lucky and have them with their breakfast. The pear trees in the walled garden seem to be set for a bumper of a crop. I'm not entirely sure who those will belong too, but as I'm the only one who routinely spends time in there with the plants I'm sure I'll manage to have a few.

The front of the greenhouse is all abloom with thyme and my strawberries are nestled amongst it. There are hundreds of bees and dozens of butterflies on it at any moment. I love visiting it in the afternoon sunshine when it seems to be busiest.

The Wild Things

My most exciting report on this front is that upon my return I have finally spotted a red squirrel and a rabbit! It seemed so weird to me that this place would be empty of them both. It was wonderful to get even a glimpse of them. The swallows that nested on the side of the house have all fledged and mostly disappeared. The little birds are coming back. Swallows must be scary!!

Last evening I was down for a swim—hot temperatures and a returning tide over the sunbaked rocks make for glorious water temperatures—and I just caught the end of what must have been quite the dramatic squabble. Three red kite (a medium sized bird of prey) were chased away from the oak trees near the garden by a group of jackdaws (crow family). Both sides of the fight were being very vocal about the whole thing and it was amazing! Also a little too fast for me to grab the camera from my backpack.

There are also a million tiny little toads everywhere. Even as I look out the window beside my desk as I'm typing I can see one little fellow hopping across the gravel drive. I had to shoo one out of the door way the other day! I've only seen one large toad, so I'll report back on how they grow and whether we're completely taken over!

All the Pretty Flowers

How could I write to you of plants from Scotland and not be excited at the first blooms of heather? As the first shy flowers started to show—pinks on the rocks nearest the sea--I knew I would be able to write to you about heather this month. As it starts to bloom with enthusiasm all around me, I find myself walking and singing this tune—first made famous I think by the Corries.

> Will you go Lassie go? (Wild Mountain Thyme)
> *Oh the summertime is coming*
> *And the trees are sweetly blooming*
> *And the wild mountain thyme*
> *Grows around the blooming heather*
> *Will ye go, Lassie go?*
> *And we'll all go together*
> *To pluck wild mountain thyme*
> *All around the blooming heather*
> *Will ye go, Lassie go?*

The fact that I already knew these songs, just starts to make so much sense these days. (If you want to hear how it sounds in my head and all the verses search for Wild Mountain Thyme—Sarah Calderwood).

The symbolism of heather varies with the colour, but I had to laugh during my research for it. Traditional purple heather like I've picked for you, is used to represent admiration, beauty, and solitude. Oh my.

Until next month,
Susie xx

AUGUST 2019

The Gardeners Cottage
Argyll's Secret Coast
Scotland, UK

August 23, 2019

Greetings my dear friends. It's such a pleasure to think about what I'm going to write to you each month and who or what I want to feature on the front of the envelopes. I have about a hundred ideas so narrowing it down to something I loved or something that is really impactful to me is a process in and of itself.

This month I have chosen the peacock butterfly who is still hanging out about the estate in great numbers—I used to be one of the last to leave a party too. They actually are native species here in the UK and stick around throughout the year. Some adults even managing to hibernate over the winter in dry spots.

But I wanted to write about one of the great immigrant butterflies, a far-travelled creature like me. A tough, tiny thing filled with ancestral DNA from this place who have made a pilgrimage of generations to be here: the Painted Lady butterfly (*vanessa cardui*). Their tale resonated

A Painted Lady butterfly on the buddleia outside the guest room.

deeply with me this month. The Painted Lady is a phenomenal creature. Each year the species makes a 7,500 mile round trip pilgrimage from sub-saharan Africa across the Mediterranean, through Europe, across the Channel, disperses throughout the UK to even the farthest northern tip of Scotland. The little butterfly flies almost 100 miles a day. It lives for only 5-8 weeks and it can take six generations to make the pilgrimage. Think of that! Six generations committed to achieving success for the species that they will never see. What if we could commit to that in our work towards repairing the damage we have done to the planet?

But that's not all, that's just an average year! Every ten years or so a magical thing happens when millions of them make it to these shores. 2019 was one of those years. Suddenly in late July and early August there were thousands of them where usually there might be 10. It was amazing to find yourself surrounded by these beautiful creatures on each path. I too have some pretty special resonance with measuring big moments by the decade. The last time the Painted Ladies descended by the millions here was the summer of 2009. My first summer in London after ten years in Seattle. Ten years later this is my first summer planted here in Scotland. To feel my own rhythms of change and growth matching another of nature's big travellers is so joyful to me. What will you do before the Painted Ladies bloom again?

About the house

August was my birthday month and I welcomed some dear friends and their children for a week. It's so much fun to have space to let kids be a bit feral. They don't have to hold your hand on the road or keep up. They aren't in danger. Toys become rocks and Tupperware used as buckets on the beach. Sandcastles get decorated with shells and feathers. It's a really magical thing. I love that I get to be the one that provides that kind of feeling.

The swing on the estate grounds became the hit of the trip. George, who is four years old, spent hours on his belly flying over the edge of the hill like a super hero. When unbidden he started to sing "A Whole New World" from Aladdin—the song about the magic carpet ride—well I might have teared up with joy a bit.

We went across Loch Fyne to Tarbert and had a birthday lunch at the Starfish restaurant that I've been waiting to try. It was wonderful! And walking onto the ferry at Portavadie as passengers makes it lots of fun and of course then everyone can have wine with lunch! We took a day trip to Oban and I was treated to a birthday present from the universe when I lost my wallet and it was turned in to the tourist centre untouched! We filled the days and I hated to see them all go, but I know they'll be back.

I turned 48 this month and I love how fast the lessons are coming these days. When you are young your lessons come quickly about how to do things and the incredible amount of world there is to explore and learn; in mid-life for me it's been lessons about why, meaning, and what's valueable. I'm learning so much having this space alone with myself to slow down and pay attention to me too.

The only thing that really concerns me about having all this incredible fertile time alone is that I may forget how to be a normal human being. Can you forget how to talk to strangers and hold a conversation? I've gone quite inward and gloriously feral myself! This area of Scotland is not very populated at all and one of the on-going concerns of the community is finding enough staff to keep businesses running. I noticed this right away and had been quietly contemplating what I felt like doing to help. Then one day on the local Tighnabruaich community Facebook page the lovely local art gallery was looking for casual help. Perfect. And as things in small places often go, I met the owner briefly and walked away with a set of keys and a date that weekend to cover. It's been a lovely little addition to my schedule. They send me dates, I help when I can, and spend days in the gallery talking about art while surrounded by beautiful things. On my first day I sold a £3,000 painting so they love me. The extra money helps and I can mostly do a lot of what I do at my desk at home!

In the Greenhouse & Around the Walled Garden

As you would expect August has been incredibly lush! I've filled your letter with pictures because I so want to share. The abundance of summer flowers had even the untended parts of the walled garden looking swoon-worthy. So many lovely surprises of asiatic lilies peeking through, daisies as tall as your shoulders, and some form of Black-eyed Susan that grew

well over my head. You can tell which plants are the hardiest and have self-propagated throughout the garden. It's also been such a lesson in the waves and timings of things. I've always been one to want things to happen and stay. Forever. I'm still in shock that walking a marathon once two decades ago didn't keep me fit for the rest of my life! But paying attention, really watching the flow of nature and the splurge of fertility and then its demise, even within the season, has been awe inspiring. It's just another call of that lesson we hear so much to stay in the present moment and enjoy the now because it can't last.

So in the meantime I filled my house with purple and blue hydrangeas. I cut vases full of the striking orange fronds of the crocosmia that grows rampant on the estate. I collected meadowsweet in the morning sunshine and made a beautifully refreshing fermented "champagne." An app I have found for my phone called "Picture This" helps immensely to identify flowers!!

I have also begun to harvest some of my own vegetables. We ate my first potatoes. My peas seemed to give me one small harvest and then go on holiday for August like the lucky people of France. The herbs continue to thrive and I'll be learning about preserving them in the next bit. The tomatoes are truly nature's masterpiece though. Capturing the taste of sunshine as perfectly as the apricots did. The pears in the walled garden are in glorious abundance. Any suggestions about what to do with them?? I have learned that you are not to let pears ripen on the tree because there they ripen from the inside out, so by the time the outside looks ripe, the inside is mush! They should be picked just as they start to show a little yellow and easily twist off the tree. So much learning! I love this phase of my education.

Yesterday I am very happy to report that I also won a significant battle about the use of herbicides around my house! Yay!!! We are creating a no-chemical zone distinct from the rest of the estate. I can't win the whole war just yet, but at least it's a start. I feel like I stood up for the part of the planet that was under my control. More to come!

All The Wonderful Creatures

The joys of all the creatures small and great are still very present for me here. On the domestic front there are some baby coos (Scottish Highland Cattle) in one of the upper pastures and sometimes they are your reward for leaving the estate. The big bullocks were found on my driveway one night and their  Houdini skills have seen them moved off to a different pasture and I've yet to find them. I miss seeing them out my kitchen window.

The songbirds had all gone mysteriously quiet and I've been trying to understand whether or not they were just off for a big quiet moult (like we all need), or their time this far north was complete and they are gone south. But the mornings have been conspicuously absent of birdsong. It doesn't feel right to have a sunny morning without all those little birds. The owls more than make up for it at night though and they have been very vocal of late! I love lying in bed with my book and hearing them call from around the cottage.

One of the biggest rewards for a twilight foray out into the garden for a walk has been finding hedgehogs. I had lived in the UK for ten years and never seen one live and wild. And once I met the first one, I couldn't stop going out to try  and spot them. They are as cute as I had hoped. Their innocence and defence perfectly matched. I posted a video of one waddling off the road in front of us and of finding the others sleeping on the paths in the walled garden. I am deeply in love and will attempt to spot as many as I can before they hibernate this year.

They are so hard to get good pictures of in that light, so I apologise to those of you who may have seen this one already on social media!

I'm sure when next I write to you I will be writing of the descent of the glories of autumn. Already I am pleading with summer to linger a while more and not leave me now. The first fog has descended, there is a single branch of golden leaves that mock my from my desk, the mythical Rowan trees are in full red berry, and the bracken is rusting from the bottom. But the sun still shines hot and is still to the north when it sets. So I am pleased when summer answers "not just yet."

"We need the tonic of wildness...At the same time that we are earnest to explore and learn all things, we require that all things be mysterious and unexplorable, that land and sea be indefinitely wild, unsurveyed and unfathomed by us because unfathomable. We can never have enough of nature."

~ Henry David Thoreau, Walden, or Life in the Woods

Much love,
Susie x

SEPTEMBER 2019

The Gardeners Cottage
Argyll's Secret Coast
Scotland, UK

September 19, 2019

My dear friends. As always,
I so enjoy collecting moments
and experiences that I want to
write to you about. It's become such a wonderful ingredient to
my daily practise of attempting to rewild this life of mine. I
have some beautiful stories to share with you this month and
some hard ones. You're here for the whole ride right? September has been quite a doozy so far! Things coming hard and fast
both in the exquisiteness of the beauty surrounding me as well
as the pain and trials.

I am currently having a very hard time with the management of the estate caused by a dispute over the stewardship of
the glasshouse. I have been working quietly and persistently
for months to get it clarified, but it looks like that is not going
to be the solution. I think the lesson I want to share with the
experience so far is how much it is teaching me to stand up
for myself and my boundaries. I have been able to navigate
this challenging situation with so much more calm than I have
ever been able to do such things before. Obviously that doesn't
mean perfection—there has still been some swearing and shaking involved! But as I was walking yesterday evening in the autumn light, that stunning rotation of degrees by which the sun
hits the planet. It's so noticeable and so damn beautiful. See
even here I digress and don't complete the sentence and I'm

not even still looking at it anymore, just thinking about the beauty of it and I lose myself.

But last night as I was walking and drinking in the beauty of the land I noticed my own happiness. I noticed the deep calm inside me that reminds me that I can navigate this however it might need to be done. That I have no responsibility other than to advocate for myself and deal with information as I receive it. That I am perfectly capable of handling it and I have no need to catastrophise any outcome. I will be fine. My dream is still happening. The story might have more twists and turns than I thought! And that's ok too. And I give so much credit for that calmness, that grounded, rooted-surety firmly to the time I've spent in nature these last few months. The calmness I have rediscovered in myself through it. Maybe that's what rewilding is.

In the sky

Right from the beginning of the month one of the most exciting things was the return of night. I know I will probably be complaining about it's grip on me as we progress into the winter, but I really noticed how happy I was to feel it's soft decent around the house before bed each night. To see the light of the stars and the moon. I had missed them more than I knew.

Very early in the month there was a brilliant clear sky and the stars could make you cry. Millions of them. The Milky Way trailing through the night like a river of glitter spilled across the table. I hadn't spent time with stars like that in a very long time. There were so many stars even the constellations that have always been my friends and guides weren't instantly distinguishable. And I realised with my change in latitude what I would be looking at would also slightly differ. I ran for my phone and my star app (I use the free iPhone App StarTracker Lite). And I discovered a gift and meaningful symbol for me. Aquila. The eagle. It's what decorates your envelope this month.

Aquila is a beautiful constellation on the celestial equator whose recording goes back to Ptolemy's original cataloguing of constellations in the second century. I had never seen it before. It was a warm night and I just stood there and learned it. Scientifically there are all sorts of lovely things about the constellation. It's in the Milky Way and the biggest star in the constellation Altair is one of the closest naked eye stars to earth. Only 17 light-years away. In contrast Polaris (the North Star) is about 433 light years away! This is my star neighbour! If you live towards the north go outside and see if you can find it.

But it's more meaningful than that. The eagle symbol is pretty important to me on this journey to be in this place and writing to you. When I started getting really serious about moving up here to Scotland I had a dream. I was standing on a beach, surrounded by hills and mountains, like many spots up here.

My dream eagle.

I was standing alone and a golden eagle flew to me and gave me a book. Being me I remembered in the dream wondering "why isn't it a sea eagle???" LOL I can't get out of the way of my brain even when I'm sleeping. The book and the eagle stayed with me. So much so that I drew the eagle. And she's here in Scotland with me. She was the start of me picking up pencils and brushes consistently again. I didn't know what the book was, but I understood my road to it was here in Scotland.

So when I was moved to tears by stars and learned they were The Eagle I was overcome with joy. A confirmation of something I don't even really know how to articulate to you.

And then there's more.

I was walking about the estate and was called to visit the little graveyard behind the main house. I had been there once before and been moved by the idea of the people who had once loved this place enough to be here for generations. I hadn't even found time to write to you about it

The small family cemetery.

yet!! But when I went back it was even more moving and I was even more curious about these people. I found myself back home down a rabbit hole of research and sketching out in my mind the story. Wanting to tell a story like theirs. I started to wonder if that might be the purpose of my being in this place. I wondered if it didn't matter if I wasn't here for the years I had hoped, if that story was what I needed most to take with me.

On the day I came to view this place I was walking what is now the familiar route down to the sea and I said to the land: I love you, I want to be here. If you want me here have them choose me and I will come. And I let it go. I went back down south and waited knowing I had asked. And they chose me.

So again I surrendered the outcome. I was asking myself questions about whether or not I'm to "do" something with this story I uncovered. And the next morning I was walking home from the sea and a golden eagle was flying over the pasture towards my house. I didn't recognise it at first. Just that often thought sentence when an eagle arrives suddenly—my that's a big bird. And as I watched it glide and heard it cry out I knew what it was and my whole body was over taken by chills.

The bounty of plants

I had a beautiful conversation with a stranger in the art gallery the other day. We were talking about the energy of autumn, the distinct gear change from summer. It's so perceptible to any that care to pay attention, but I'd never heard anyone articulate it in exactly the way he did and I loved it. He said the tangibility of autumn is in the quiet. Empty streets, but lights on in the kitchen quiet. The end of the work day-feet up feeling while your dinner is cooking. All the outward energy in nature of growing and flowering and collecting and spreading and nurturing stops. There's a full stop and that energy is missing. Of course it is! Why hadn't I ever thought of that before! Imagine what the energy of all that action puts into the world! Autumn is when the output stops. So we harvest the gifts of the previous season and say good luck to seeds and roots having a private journey until we hear from them again in the spring. Marvellous.

Cobnuts or wild hazelnuts are plentiful on the estate and I collected some, but left lots for the squirrels.

The harvest here has turned to pears, apples, hazelnuts, blackberries, and tomatoes. Am I the only one who basically just eats fresh cherry tomatoes off the vine by the handful instead of cooking something? I've been living off of Spanish tomato bread with my sourdough and all the other gorgeous plunder. I've been so happy. If you've never travelled to Spain it's a simple and delicious recipe. Basically you toast bread—I do it in a griddle pan, but I'm sure it works with traditional toasting too. You politely rub the bread with garlic, and then basically squeeze the insides of a really ripe tomato onto the bread. Drizzle with olive oil and a little salt and pepper. Then swoon with happiness. In fact I'm going to go eat some right now. It should be called Sunshine Toast.

So picture me delightfully peeling pears and apples. Putting pies in the freezer for later. Making too many crumbles for myself and spending a portion of most walks picking fresh blackberries and cobnuts too. Alfred has become very, very patient with the berry picking and now understands that I'm going to stop a lot. It's so uniquely satisfying though to leave your house for a walk and come home with pockets full of food.

This strange fruit is Medlar. It was really popular when the Romans were in Britain. It comes into its own after a frost and therefore was useful for having something sweet longer into the winters. There are two medlar trees in the orchard by the steading.

When I say it's been a difficult month it has been on so many levels. I had a really traumatic incident happen one evening in the first week of the month. Alfred and I came round the corner of the glasshouse into the walled garden after our evening walk. It was a really windy day coming in from the north and it was a relief to get behind the wall. We weren't the only ones who thought that and we startled the two little roe deer that are always about the house. They jumped up to run off, but the doe panicked and went the wrong way. She ran straight into the metal garden gate and shoved her head between the rails. Where it got stuck.

She started thrashing and pulling and screaming. The buck disappeared. Alfred wasn't helping. I tied him at first to see if I could help her quickly. When it became obvious I couldn't I had to take him to the house and try to find something to bend the iron gate. The poor girl. She was stuck in there for quite a long time while I tried different things. I tried to hold her calm to keep her from breaking her neck. I finally scavenged a pipe and was able to get her free. We stood there for a minute me with a bent pipe, extensive bruising on my hands, arms and legs from trying to hold her still. Her with injuries unknown. She managed to walk away and then jumped the fence and was gone by the time I was back from putting the pipe away. I was so scared that she might have broken her jaw or done other such damage and wouldn't live anyway. It was devastating and traumatising. All week after I would look at the bruises on my hands and say—as I heal she heals. Needless to say they haven't been back and I probably won't ever know if she made it.

That encounter was followed by a devastating reminder of the climate crisis we are living in. I'm so surrounded here by wildlife and plants and nature having her way to more of an extent than most places. But that doesn't mean I can forget about the rest of the world. That story was brought home to the shore just down the loch a few days ago. First it was a joyful thing. A mother and baby sowerby's beaked whales. They were jumping in the waters just off the shore and people were delightfully reporting their appearance. It was very strange to see them here. Then later this week it became obvious why they were here. They were starving. They baby beached itself and the mother followed. She was rescued while the coast guard and wildlife agency tried to help the baby. She kept re-beaching herself and they were eventually both euthanised due to their poor condition.

We must do more to reverse the damage we have done to the world. I sat on my little rock edge as I do each morning and counted the fisherman's nets out in the loch. I thought of the starving whales and mostly just couldn't handle my grief for what we've done. I need to continue to find more and more ways to personally address over-consumption and to support law change that prioritises the environment. We can't go on this way.

September has been a tough month. But all is not lost. This month also millions of people, led by the youngest among us with the most to lose, showed up to protest around the world against the inaction of governments in regards to climate change. The world is both extremely beautiful and in deep crisis. I am extremely worried and more happy than I've been in a long time. All these things can be true at the same time. Finding our way to both be active about things we care about and care for ourselves at the same time is perhaps the challenge of our times.

As always, I relish the opportunity to share my experience with you. I'm headed south for a week or so to see some friends and have an annual weekend in Paris at their most famous horse race. It will be wonderful. But a part of me will be wondering how much the light and colours will change while I'm gone and feel like I'm missing out.

Until next month.
Much love,
Susie xx

OCTOBER 2019

The Gardeners Cottage
Argyll's Secret Coast
Scotland, UK

October 18, 2019

Dear friends it goes so fast
sometimes, the time between
letters! I feel like I just wrote
yesterday, but in fact I was travelling away from the Cottage
for two weeks at the end of last month and that made time disappear completely. I was down south emptying a closet in my
flat for my renters to have a bit more space—I now have a suit-
case full of formal gowns here so prepare to randomly dress for
dinner if you visit! I did some dog-sitting, some babysitting,
and caught up with friends before spending an annual weekend in Paris with other dear friends. We attend a horse race
there at the racecourse called Longchamp (yes the handbags
are named after it!) but mostly we catch up on life, drink champagne and eat beautiful food together. It's one of my favourite
weekends of the year and one of the few things I think would
get me away at this time. I was so worried I would return and
all the leaves would have fallen and I would have missed it all!
I didn't at all. It's been glorious watching which type of tree
and in which locations turn first. It's definitely been birch then
beech so far. Oak well behind.

I think in reality the break was good. As I told you last
month things were a bit difficult and I was having to really
fight my ground for clarity of my situation here. I am writing
to you from my chair inside the sunny greenhouse today. My
sunny greenhouse. Agreed to be a material part of the cottage

and for my exclusive use. Whew. So all the drama that ensued from my holding my ground was completely unnecessary and I am relieved. I now need to buy myself a tall ladder and some extending pruners! The apricot tree and the grapes have run wild out the closing top and need to be trimmed. I've been trying to borrow the equipment from the estate for months, but now I'm just going to buy it and get it done. Imperfect zero waste! Sometimes you just need some tools!

My proposal for taking over the walled garden was declined and I imagine it will take some time to rebuild relations with the estate manager who behaved so badly before the final information came down. It's amazing how people with the tendency to bully deploy that tactic their whole life. But I'm very relieved and have a secure base again to start building this life.

I've noticed something really important though in these first few weeks back with things settled. I realised where my peace lives. Because it was sure missing. Even in these beautiful surroundings. I realised I have systematically removed every external barrier to my peace. No more 15 story construction project beside me. No more threats of people popping in and out of my greenhouse and dictating how that space will feel. No more boss to please. No more expectations to answer to. I have purposely stripped away almost all the external things that were impacting my peace and happiness. And there has been a price to pay for that, I'm more financially unstable than I have been since University. But I've been so willing to risk it for peace and creativity. So you can imagine how confused I was to find that it wasn't paying off. The fight had been fought and it was over and I wasn't feeling at all peaceful.

I was walking the dog on this beautiful land obsessing about what was missing, what I couldn't do, what wasn't available to me. What would be perfect. I realised that I wasn't working on the one part that rules all of my peace: my thoughts. There was no peace there. Obsessing about what wasn't happening was freezing me from taking the action I could because I was so attached to this idea that there was a perfect action which would be better. It was just another way for my brain to slip me out of the present moment, where I could make decisions and take actions, into some future-perfect conditions or circumstances that did not exist. And the funny thing about the future or might-have-been scenarios is that they don't yet exist and you can't take a single action from there. You can't maximise your enjoyment of what you have. You can't start building a bridge to a different future from that fictitious place in time. You can't enjoy the peace of the moment and the gifts of today. Peace within me exists in the present moment. I can only feel it when I'm here and not letting my head take me into worrying about what could happen, or revisiting what already has happened. I am so fortunate to be in this place on the planet and I was squandering it. But I caught myself. May I always catch myself. May I do it quickly and with good humour. I'll report back on how it's going.

About the house

I've finally been able to add in a full dining room table that I had been staring at for a few months at the local charity shop in Dunoon. It seats 8 and although they sold one of the carver chairs separately (grrrr) I got the rest for £50. It's beautiful wood, generous seats, extendable, and I'm looking forward to it as a re-

upholstery project come short winter days. I'll share the whole process when I get started, but for now at least there will be a proper table for Christmas dinner!

Funds have been tight for the last few months so I haven't been able to 'just go get' the pieces that are still needed even from charity shops. It's a fascinating experience really. Moving so slowly. I did some consulting work last month to catch up the bills, but the reality of me not being able to continue too much more in that space is clear. Completely changing your life is hard! I haven't done it with a nest egg, and I have been so fortunate as to be able to rely on some friends when emergency car repairs struck this month. Your contributions via Patreon are so wonderful and each month I take the profit (after stamps, paper, and ink) and add something to the house that's needed. So your contribution truly goes into building this adventure with me and I'm so grateful to have you along. Thank you.

The Creatures

As always there is much to report on this front! And it adds to my happiness so much to have so many creatures close. All of the animals have eluded my camera though this month, so my drawing and description will have to do!

The autumn rutting season has been in full force for the Red Deer stags. This is the time of year that they fight with each other for the right to mate with the hinds (female red deer). Standing outside in the evening listening to them bellow their challenge to any comers is such an amazing sound. Full grown males can weigh up to 350 kg and are the 4th largest deer species in the world. You can picture the stags standing on a ridge in the hills behind the house, their magnificent antlers tilted back, feeling as invincible as it's possible to feel, and sounding their calls up and down the loch. It's old and wonderful and things in my body respond to it deeply.

I see mostly hind on the estate, despite hearing so many stags this month. I startled two this morning coming out the door, and it's an amazing thing to have gotten used to the sound of them thundering away across the lawn if you pop out in the dark to look at the stars or let the dog out. The come and eat the beech nuts from the trees. It's not really safe to have the dog out in the dark during the rut as the stags can be really aggressive, so we've adjusted our routine quite a bit.

The bird I've drawn on your envelope this month is the grey heron. There are so many here on the estate that a day doesn't go by without my usually encountering at least one. I've become so fond of their heavy, prehistoric looking bodies in flight above  me. They aren't interested in a close relationship, but the bounty of the gardens, ponds, and shore seems to let them thrive here. After I painted the envelopes I started researching their symbolic meaning and was delighted. It was all about stillness and tranquility. A sense of independence and the lessons of time alone. Sacred serenity. And understanding patience and stillness for recognising opportunity. Swoon! How lovely.

And I'm so pleased to report that all the little birds are back! Every kind of tit—blue, great, coal—are back to flittering about outside my windows. I can tell you it costs me time in the afternoon at the computer when I should be getting on with work things and I'm just staring at them or trying to have the camera ready when one decides to come straight to the window to collect a bug! I've not managed yet, but will show you when I do get the shot!

The birds all elude my iPhone for great photos. And I haven't managed one of our newly arrived neighbours! A pair of swans have taken up residence in the pond in the cattle pasture. They are often down in one of the bays on the loch fishing and paddling about as well. I'm not sure of their plans to settle, but it's wonderful to see the flash of white or watch them come in to land on the pond out my windows.

Other things

"I'm so glad to live in a world where there are Octobers."
~ LM Montgomery

October has been the month of rainbows. The first days I was home I saw at least one a day. I saw my first dawn rainbow. There were double rainbows. Partial rainbows. Ones that ended in the sea and others which ended just behind the house. That lovely mix of the sunlight pouring in now at oblique angles instead of the steady overhead push of summer and fast-moving showers earlier in the month made conditions glorious. What a treat!

The last few days have been clear and sunny. The temperature has dropped and that means our first real frost this morning, a chilly house, and slippers becoming precious accessories again. It's astonishing though to remember the effect that frosty conditions have on the air quality, even here where it's already so good. It was positively crystal clear this morning. Like any soot or dust or other things floating in the air had all been momentarily weighed down overnight and just the crispy best air was left to savour. Standing on our edge of the loch I heard the church bells ringing 10am from Tarbert for the first time ever. More than five miles across the water. It was extraordinary.

November will be a busy month here at the cottage as I have visitors almost every week! Three sets from North America!!! And one dear friend from London coming up to help plan our

Christmas-week festivities. I'm trying to get in the mood to clean the house that many times! Hahahahahaha it feels like the holidays already with that.

Writing these letters to you each month is such medicine for my soul and a reliable spark for my creativity. As I try to digest the things that have happened the last month, get excited during my day when there is something I want to share with you, a piece of beauty spotted, another bit of wildness returned to my heart, I am overcome with gratitude for the opportunity. Thank you for letting me write to you.

I hope your October has been filled with plenty and that we all look forward to the joys November might offer.

Much love,
Susie xx

NOVEMBER 2019

The Gardeners Cottage
Argyll's Secret Coast
Scotland, UK

November 19, 2019

Dearest friends,

Oh my what a month so far! Thank goodness that I need to write before the month concludes because I can already tell this might be the chattiest letter so far. November has been the nicest

The drive down to the cottage turns into a lovely autumn tunnel.

whirlwind. It's a month I expected everything to be in retreat and slow and dark and that's true, but it's definitely not the whole truth. Those of you who have been with me since the beginning, or have taken advantage of the letter archive on the Patreon page, will know that each month so far I basically mourn the ending of some stage of nature and am pleasantly shocked by the arrival of the next one. It goes on that way. I'm pretty sure this is a significant portion of rewilding my life. Remembering that nature when left to her own pace will also delight you and you don't have to force things quite as hard as we have been led to believe. Each of the delights are so different and come from the ending of the cycles of what came before. The daffodils and bluebells of spring to the summer bounty of flowers and blooms of butterflies to the autumn fecundity of the harvest all nuts and seeds and final ripening of fruits. Now winter is arriving with it's own stunning beauty and I am humble enough to begin the understanding that my role here is watching. Documenting. Noticing. Relearning. We have become so resistant to the ending of cycles in our daily lives. We are completely attached to the indefinite prolonging of some pleasures not trusting that which is out of our control and just beyond the current type of beauty.

The Trees

The pear tree in the walled garden turns a vibrant red.

Surely in this month of deep autumn the trees need a heading of their own! It has been wonderful to watch the trees change and the leaves fall on the estate. The birches went first, the beeches followed and the oaks were last to start to change.

At the beginning of the month you couldn't turn your head a fraction without encountering a new autumnal scene that made you gasp. The oaks started to drop enormous acorns wantonly across the roads and their leaves turned such a beautiful yellow. The little trees that make our tunnel across the road into the estate turned it into a perfect dappled portal. I discovered that pear trees turn the most gorgeous colour even after giving such a gift of delicious fruit. The squirrels have been very busy and I've finally started to see the red squirrels on a regular basis as they collect their stores. Each day I walked and noticed the small variations in colour and the growing piles of leaves on the ground. And then a stormy Monday a week or so ago saw most of them gone and leaving a new beautiful transparency to the sky and views. Their timely conclusion letting more of the precious light fall to warm the ground.

The most exquisite thing to report I have no photographic proof of occurring! How often do I walk without my phone??? It was a sunset that looked a lot like this one. The water was still and calm and I had wandered to the picnic table overlooking the loch to take in the show. The seals gave the most exquisite surprise performance! Imagine them all in perfect silhouette against the orange of the setting sun. In the quiet I heard a splash off the edge of the beach and looked over to see them racing and leaping out of the water with every thrust. First two together dashing from one island to the edge of the beach, then another between the islands. Then another and another. Jumping, flying, splashing. Zooming around the bay and appearing to delight in their own acrobatic abilities. The birds settling in to roost for the dark provided the orchestral accompaniment and it was the most beautiful thing to witness. I might not have a photograph, but I think it has joined some other magical moments that I can close my eyes and recall perfectly.

The deer rut season has concluded and evening forays outdoors are no longer accompanied by the calling of stags. Things have returned to normal and mostly we surprise the red deer eating the beech nuts on the lawn west of the house. Alfred had one merry chase the other night and we returned to the house just before bed with mud up to his elbows and scenes to dream about for days.

The first pheasant shoots have happened on the estate now, with several more to come. I have to say that this particularly British way of doing it is incredibly unpalatable to me. Basically, as I have observed it here, they have a human feed young birds for months to grow them. They put far too many of the species on the land (hundreds here) in order to ensure there are enough for the shoots. They kill as many potential predators as possible in the surrounding areas—lamping foxes at night and shooting them and putting up snares around the bird feeding stations. Then on the day the 15 or so "shooters" come stand in various locations around the estate while humans drive the birds over their heads in order for them to shoot. It's like playing a video game with sentient beings. I'm not opposed to hunting. I eat meat and have enjoyed eating pheasant. But this is stacking the game in unconscionable ways. There is no luck. No chance. No skill. No effort on behalf of the hunter. The tweed shooting outfits and the truckloads of beautiful retrievers are lovely scenes. But I think we know better than this now. Just go for a damn walk and find a wild bird on your own. End of rant. I've been keeping a collection of the feathers I find on my walks to incorporate them into an outdoor Christmas wreath to remember their loud, clucky presence and the joy their beautiful plumage brings.

The swans that made an appearance last month left and then another set appeared! They appeared just after the full moon on a frosty morning and looked like a fairytale out in the pond. During a little scramble along the coast one large one flew over us and it was amazing to see the scale of them in flight. It also gave me an opportunity to see some additional identification features and I have learned that they are Whooper Swans, the European equivalent of the Trumpeter Swan. They are on the Amber list of conservation (meaning there are threats but are not specifically protected at the moment). The Whooper Swan is one of the heaviest flying birds in the world. It's stunning to see. They make the long journey from their summer breeding grounds in Iceland to winter in the UK. It seems like the estate might make a lovely rest stop as they all stay for about a week and disappear just when I get my hopes up! Now I know their story though I'll wish them safe onwards journey to their winter homes and hope to see them when they return again in spring.

The pleasure of guests

November has brought the most guests yet to visit me at the cottage. Five separate visits, three completed as I write to you. I love the house full. I love walking people around the estate and surprising them with all the wonders. Everyone has different feelings and attraction to different parts of the estate. I love seeing which it will be. I love seeing what animals will show themselves.

Friends since our university days in Saskatoon have the standard guestbook photo "In bed with Alfred."

I love the weather that comes and the understanding that for some we can range afield and others need the permission of a soggy day to just deeply rest. This month we've went on starlit walks and scavenging greens from the forestry for wreath making. We tried new restaurants. Did beautiful rituals. Had a twilight walk surrounded by bats and getting a glimpse of the big owl that everyone hears and few of us see! There were cozy fires, hot water bottles and a lot of very good sports when the boiler first began to misbehave and then broke entirely leaving us without heat for portions of their stay! You forget all the skills you have for coping without heat for short periods. Lots of baking and huddling in the kitchen! The estate manager has brought round some space heaters that have been a life saver! And the electric shower in the guest bath, usually a source of mediocrity in terms of heat, became a refuge. Thank you Emily and Katharine for enjoying it so much here even without heat that you became subscribers to these letters!

But the best part of the visits is always the conversations and the rekindling of friendships from somewhere else coming back to life in this space and landscape. It's always such a pleasure to have strands of your life rewoven into your present. And I revel in the fact that this place is so capable of bringing magic and joy to my guests too. Each guest has brought me a little specific magic and all of them reminded me of one of my most important goals for living here was to invite others in to experience it too.

All who visit must introduce themselves to the standing stones.

I already have two lovely patrons booked in for stays next year! (Sienna & Susan, Jan & Graham I'm so excited to see you!)

Sunset viewpoints with a thermos and Alfred for warmth.

Even if you never make it in person, I'm always so thrilled to share this place with you in these letters. I love hearing how you settle and slow down to read them. I want you to know how much pleasure that gives me. Please don't be shy about emailing, messaging or writing back! I love hearing from you and I love the global magic we are making. The connection between us through these little letters is already moving around the world. A special welcome to the first Australian patron this month! Thank you Ann! Together we're making our own little ripples of rest and presence and a little appreciation of awe in the world and that seems like a good use of time to me.

Other things

The earth is hardened many mornings now by the frost and the beauty of the decoration by it on the leaves and lichen is thrilling. The other morning driving Katharine to meet the bus the sun on the frost made the whole world a sparkly wonderland. The cold temperatures were brought on by clear skies and the star gazing was spectacular and I find myself dragging my guests outside wrapped in blankets to just try to take it all in. We're always so glad after we do that. So November has been bringing its own unique magic. A month of waving goodbye to some and welcoming others.

I have a new mantra for a chilly, old Scottish cottage in winter—if you start to get cold, just go outside for a walk and the house will feel toasty upon your return. If that fails have a delicious hot bath and snuggle with a hot water bottle and one of the wool blankets scattered around the house. The smoky little fire can be revved up for ambience if not terribly good for warmth and thus the march to winter pleasures begins. Honestly I have learned my lessons and am curious about what joys each month will bring. It won't be July joys in December, but I trust that the December joys will be extraordinary. I can't wait to share them with you.The rest of the month is filled with Christmas prep and learning to adjust my days to the new schedule of available light.

"I'n November the trees are standing all sticks and bones. Without their leaves, how lovely they are, spreading their arms like dancers."

~ Cynthia Rylant, In November

Much love,
Susie xx

DECEMBER 2019

The Gardeners Cottage
Argyll's Secret Coast
Scotland, UK

December 7, 2019

Dearest friends,

Due to the post being over-whelmed this time of year—as you can imagine there is nothing I like better than getting cards in the mail so I'm not complaining—I wanted to get your card and letter off as

Nature's fairy lights are abundant here and are often prisms making them appear in all sorts of colours.

early as possible. That means the cottage isn't completely decorated yet for Christmas (what I sort of celebrate, but really it's more like a Solstice/Saturnalia/Christmas mash-up that leans towards wonderful food, boozy, compulsive approaches to finishing a puzzle that's always harder than it looks, friends and country walks). So I'll send you some pictures of that in January if it turns out special!

Because the cards need to be off so early I thought I would just include a short note about what I've been thinking about lately. The weather has been crispy, clear, and cold for most of my time with guests and then today turned to warm and wet. Really wet. There's a lovely yellow blob flashing "rain warning" over my part of Scotland on the weather page for the next 24 hours. I took Alfred out early for a walk and a soaking so that we'd get it over with and could spend the rest of the day being happy to be inside. I'm not sure if it's a sound theory, but it's mine. Hahaha

The landscape colours have all gone a deep bronze like this bark and the rotting bracken.

I then spent a couple of hours in the glasshouse clearing off the remaining plants: tomatoes, cucumbers, and potatoes. My plan to extend the growing season was really compromised by my time away at the end of September. The hot weather and my rudimentary watering system just caused a bit too much stress and everyone has well given up by this point. Although the potatoes who hadn't flowered both produced a few more spuds for one more meal so that was a bonus joy in the work. I pulled the roots and worked up all the potting soil. Mixing it and placed it in some of the big containers for storage until I get started with the growing season. Someone had thrown out a heavy, but hole-ridden wool blanket that I grabbed out of the bins the other day and I've cut it up to use as covers to prevent weeds. (You can do that on paths too—way better than plastic). There's a propagating table (basically a heated mini-greenhouse) in the glasshouse so I'm going to try to be quite ambitious starting things and perhaps even manage to grow some plants to sell next spring. But that's an ambition for January!

And while I walk and work with my hands I usually have some of my clearest thoughts or understanding of things I might have been struggling with at my desk. What really struck me this morning is how committed I am to my own sense of timing right now. The winter work in the glasshouse isn't yet done and what I have done someone else could have done weeks ago. And I don't care. When I moved up here I made a commitment to myself to do this without hurting myself. Hurting myself by overworking, doing things because I felt I had to not because I wanted to, overburdening myself emotionally, etc. I have never in my 48 years done things just because I wanted to. I did what was expected. I did what made people like or respect me. I did what I thought was what you were supposed to do. And I was always devastated when it was wrong or I didn't feel enough love to fill the hole I had created by not caring for myself and making myself do it anyway. Because I had given so much away of myself to do it, I felt cheated. And because I am stubborn and didn't allow myself to be wrong, for years I just did more and bigger instead of figuring out what was really happening.

What this exquisite time here at the cottage so far has taught me is that I'm the only person who can change that. So instead of bending to external pressure I let myself find my perfect time. I let myself remember what I want to do and why the effort is worth it. I let myself remember that I'm worth it! Worth having the life I dreamed about. Worth having beautiful surroundings. Worthy regardless of mistakes I make or timings I don't meet. No one else is going to figure out how to be me. No one else is going to figure out how to give what I have to give to myself and the world. And maybe I've had to be a bit drastic (or dramatic, I'm a Leo) about doing it because the only way I could even fathom how to start was to break away from almost everything else. Maybe other people don't have to do that, but this is my story and I've given myself the permission to go for it. And I can't think of a more special way to be ending the decade. To be already deep into this work of becoming more and more myself every day. I didn't even know to wish this for myself last year. I hope this last decade has brought you closer to yourself too.

My warmest wishes for a brilliant December for you and all that you love. See you in the new year!

Xx

Susie

JANUARY 2020

The Gardeners Cottage
Argyll's Secret Coast
Scotland, UK

January 17, 2020

Happiest of new year and new decade to you dear friends!

For many this month will be your first proper letter from me at the cottage and I hope you enjoy what's been happening and what's been on my mind. For those who've been with me a while already, I am so happy to be writing to you again. Our little community is now 50 letters strong and going to five countries! It's such a thrill to have it resonate so far.

As for January, just when I thought it was going to be all gentle returning of the light and poking about for emerging buds, we've been hit with some wintery weather that made time outdoors more difficult. I've been ever so grateful for the glasshouse and ways to be almost outside when the rain and the wind aren't being overly cooperative. But it's left lots of time for musing beside the fire too. I talk a lot about this being a 're-rooting' process for me and I wanted to write to you about how I found my way here to the Gardeners Cottage.

An ancestral longing for place

Like many I've been thinking a lot since I wrote you last about the last decade and the change it brought me. In 2009 I left my nice life and job in Seattle to emigrate to the United

Kingdom. I did it without a job, not very much personal re-
sources, or a clear idea of what was next for me. I just knew
that it was necessary and despite the fear or rationalisations, I
came. One action at a time I magically landed in a flat, my flat,
in London's Lancaster Gate with my darling old dog Sam and a
few lovely friends nearby to help me start weaving a real life
there.

> *"Like the first August swallow fidgeting on the tele-*
> *phone wires, we know there is something we should be*
> *doing. We know there is a Journey we should be under-*
> *taking. We cannot rest; we cannot sleep. Something in*
> *us knows that there is somewhere we should be going.*
> *And in the end, whether or not we think we can, we go*
> *because we must. We go, on a wing and a prayer, be-*
> *cause to stay is to die."*
> ~ Sharon Blackie, If Women Rose Rooted

I thought surely this is it. This is that big gesture required
of me that would unlock all my happiness and my striving and
searching would be over. But it wasn't. Because I wasn't always
solving for the right answer. I made so many new soul-friends
and had experiences normalised that I had only dreamed of before. I had adventures and explorations and it was wonderful.
But it wasn't the whole answer. Each time I have moved as an
adult I have taken it as an opportunity to pivot, to leave behind
parts of myself that I didn't want to carry to the future. It was
a good practise and helped me immeasurably. But in this last
decade I started to get the whisper that I no longer needed to
focus on pruning. I needed to learn how to stop shaping myself for any external idea of what my value might be. What did
I want to build? Who did I want to be? Where did I want to create it? How did I want to feel as I did it? Those became the more

important questions than what is my job? How much do I get paid? What are the perks? etc.

I realised I was always making my way here. Not just to the landscape of Scotland specifically, but to how I feel here. To a world I am finally creating in myself that feels like home. The permission to root myself deeply and learn to do it in these circumstances without attachment to permanence, or attachment to ownership and control—and you know I've been fighting my tendencies for these ones!

Despite the stormy weather the gorse has flowered along the loch. Besides a connection with the sun, gorse is identified with a sense of industriousness, intelligence and stringent independence. Funny how I keep noticing plants with this mythology!

I've been thinking so much about ancestral longing. Those of us with missing roots from our families recent emigrations away from the places the building materials of our very bodies spent centuries. I think ancestral longing is rampant in the children, grandchildren, great grandchildren, etc of the colonial settler immigrations to North America, Australasia, and Africa. We cling so tightly to our identities and connection to the old places, but we often also begrudge more recent immigrants for doing the same. That always saddens me. But I got curious about the longing itself.

The engineered waterfall for the old mill area down towards the cottage.

My longing for Scotland was real. I wanted to put my feet here. I wanted to stay. We often have so much longing for the old stories and words and it's been built into our people's leaving from the beginning. Think of the towns around you that are names of this place. I can't drive down the road or look at a map of Scotland without being transported to places I know from Canada and the US. Australia too. Now knowing this Scottish landscape and small villages or islands that find themselves suddenly with a mirrored existence in the middle of the wide, frozen Saskatchewan plains, I can only picture the people most often forced from their homeland and families by economic pressure or policies like the Highland Clearances renaming their new places from their longing for here. It's impossible that we their descendants wouldn't carry that feeling onwards in us. I believe that until we collectively acknowledge and heal the wounds created from this historical uprooting we won't be able to make room in the story for others suffering from what we haven't named in ourselves. We long for more of our story. We know there are missing pieces. Knowing more of the story is why we love online DNA testing so much!

The traumatic conditions of most of the colonial immigrant experience was never going to foster relationship with the land people found themselves in. The narrative was always how to make this land like the land I left. And it will never do. There is never satisfaction with what is because it is not what was. And we long for the songs and the plaids and the way a mist feels on your face. But that too is deceptive because all the emotions that went into this idea of place was because of relationships people had with this land as itself. And that's what we long for, that's where the magic lives, not in its trappings. We long for our connection with the earth and the partnership that our ancestors knew. Not because we should be living in the past, but for what they had in the past. That's what I'm learning is at the bottom of my longing.

So here I am a very lucky type of immigrant. Not here for extraction or escape from horrible things, but of my own choice. To heal some of the wounding of those who were forced to go. I think it's important to come back to this place as we are, metaphorically or physically, knowing that time hasn't stood still for either of us, but to get to know each other again, like the first days after a long absence. The myths and stories and landscape shapes serve as the old familiar jokes that ease you back into intimacy with a part of yourself. I think that's what rerooting is and why it doesn't need to be tied to one particular cottage. Rerooting is the act of remembering parts of ourselves who had a centuries-long history intertwined with a landscape beyond its simple cultivation. And no matter where we find ourselves we can use those remembered parts to come to a relationship with the earth and magic again. We can come to it whole and curious and not simply trying to make it conform to our idea of something that was lost to us.

So come home. Listen to the pipes. Let them make you cry. Stand in a spot where the echo sounds familiar to you even though it's your first visit. Greet the trees and stones with acknowledgement of what they have seen and known. Believe in fairies and sing to the selkies.

Remember that this is what your people can do. And then, if you have another place on the planet that is home now find them, their form and their names where you are. You get to keep it this time. And you keep it in the every day interactions with the other beings that are our

Snow on the hills across Loch Fyne from the standing stones.

roommates on this great planet whether it's a flower on your windowsill or the river you cross every day in your car.

In the Glasshouse

My everyday is filled with walking and noticing and working away on my plans for the new growing season. Mostly I am keeping on with short spurts of general tidying and selective pruning of the vines and trees in the glasshouse. This month I should finally be able to buy a ladder so I can finish the highest bunch. I've also started washing the windows on the inside. There is so much satisfaction in that I can't even tell you. But it's a big messy job so I'm taking it in sections on days when it is warm enough for them to dry quick and Alfred is really dirty and also needs hosing and drying! Haha.

My biggest win by far is my successful propagating of two elder cuttings. I'm so thrilled. If you've been around for a while you'll remember that weirdly there is only one elder tree near the cottage and that means my share is a very limited amount of flowers and berries (the birds get the rest). So I'll keep you posted if the spring sunshine brings them on to flower!

I've also started cuttings of my beautiful purple geranium that ha been having a very happy winter on my bedroom windowsill. I thought since it loved the spot so much the chances of the cuttings doing well there too was pretty good! So far so good.

I'm trying to wrap my head around what's possible this season for growing veg to eat. I think February will see me start many plants in the propagating table and perhaps even take a table in March at the local producers market. We'll see. I'm not terribly confident about that, but first I must successfully grow the plants!

The Creatures

My favourite thing about the last month has to be the little birds. True to the description in all the books, the little ones have formed these massive gangs of a hundred plus and when they swoop by the cottage now it's en masse. Although there is always a few outliers. My gangs seem to be made up predominantly of Blue Tits and Chaffinches. I have spotted a few Long-tailed, Coal and Great Tits too. Even with all the wind on my walks I am starting to hear their little voices again and it makes me so happy.

The lone Whooper swan wintering from Iceland in the pond has been one of my favourite morning sights while I wait for my coffee. We have only one more pheasant and partridge shoot scheduled on the estate at the end of the month. I can't wait for it to be over and to reclaim ac-

I spent the month sneaking up on swans attempting to get photos.

cess to our longer walks on the estate and more off leash time for Alfred. Although he has taken to chasing the Red Deer off into the wilderness now (I surreptitiously break the leash rules early in the morning or in the evening which of course is also prime deer time). One night the lawn was full when we popped out around 10pm. Pitch black. No moon. Me with no shoes. Alfred was off and over the ridge. About 10 minutes into it he gave me one clear ringing Old English Sheepdog bark for "how do I get back to you?" I yelled and a few minutes later he came tumbling out of the forest up to his chest in mud. You can imagine how pleased I was to be giving him a bath at that time of night!

Whether the weather be fine...

It's been blowing a hooley as they say here for the last week or so. Storm Brendan hit the northwest of the UK quite strong with wind gusts up to 90 mph further to the north. Here at the cottage I haven't had a day without about 25 mph winds at some point for ages. The old rotted fascia on one end of the cottage was a victim to it, but was quickly patched up until the spring brings more gentle times for full repair. So far we've seemed to only lose a couple more tree friends. A little holly that was growing next to an oak along the path and a bigger tree in the woodland on the entry to the estate. So lucky I think.

But it has also brought, finally, the repair of the radiators in my living room and I can finally say there is a decent heat source there! For those of you who have visited this winter before this was sorted I thank you for your grit and willingness to wear layers. The radiator next to my desk is finally doing the job of keeping my toasty while I write you, or stare out the window at the birds.

But the sun has broken through now and I need to take Alfred for a bit of a romp after being so patient with all the workmen here this morning. In the month ahead I'm looking forwards to my first Burns Night Supper here at a local community hall. I have no idea what to expect besides the poetry and some whisky! I will report back!

Much love,
Susie xx

A winter sunrise. It's the only time of
year I catch them!

The Gardeners Cottage
Argyll's Secret Coast
Scotland, UK

February 22, 2020

Winter greetings dear friends.

The real twisty trees on the mound behind the standing stones that are so magical in their reaching and bending in the wind.

When I chose the artwork for this month's envelopes I actually worried that all my news would be of spring and that it wouldn't suit. I couldn't have been more wrong. (The image on the envelope is based on a piece by Natasha Whittaker, an artist from Cornwall who gave me permission to replicate my version of it for you, and it was the first I saw that captured how it felt to look at the trees here on the estate and I knew I had to try). February has indeed been the kind of month that sculpts the trees of our landscape to bend and reach and find balance in the midst of so much pressure. In the end I think I've found myself acting much the same way, trying to find balance in the buffeting.

We've had winds of over 50 mph for at least a portion of every day if not all of it for at least three weeks. A Storm Ciara was followed within days by Storm Dennis and apparently Storm Ellen is feeling left out and looms off in the Atlantic. I never expected to be so discombobulated by wind. I grew up on the open prairies of Saskatchewan with its ever-present blow! But February has been a trial for me in unexpected ways. How long can you batten down the hatches? How long can life and work be stalled waiting for better conditions?

What has to be done anyway and how does it feel to do it? I've been finding out the answers this month and it's been uncomfortable. I've hidden from hail storms behind trees only to be driven to run for home anyway by thunder and lightning strikes at the same time. There has been never ending hail. The skies between the squalls have been incredible and rainbows still get made! But it feels like I've been on high alert for the entire month.

All of this discomfort and beauty is part I think of the rewilding of myself journey. I noticed last week when I was in the city for an airport run how much further away the weather felt. The way that the city buildings offer protection from the wind and pavement and drainage systems make the run-off disappear without getting the sense of the volume of water moving to the sea like the swelling burn which runs beside the cottage. The way the snow looks so pretty on the distant mountains versus climbing over them on a one lane road in a white out. It just woke me up to another level of privilege I am experiencing here with this life choice—the one of having a first degree relationship with nature again in all her moods, even the tough ones.

At the same time spring is so ready to burst forth. Daffodils by the thousands wait for a little prolonged warm to open their faces. A few of the brave way-showers have already done so and be damned the hail. The snow drops cling to the sides of the burn and cozy under trees. The elder trees have cautiously budded, but not opened. I so hope they all get a few gentler days soon to take over the landscape and share the joy they are saving up.

*Invitations in the winter
landscape*

The winter landscape had
me quite excited in the period
before the mad dashing about
caused by the storms. The
bracken has died away and is
beaten down. Sight lines are
at their maximum so views
are clearer and wider than they will be at any other time of the
year. Paths have emerged that just weren't noticeable in the
lushness of spring and summer. I spent the week after returning from a trip to the south walking adjacent to my usual roads,
but deeply different. Trusting the deer to make their way
safely through the wetness and ridges, which they always do. I
was treated to a sweet little meadow I didn't know and a way
to the wilder bit of the coast without having to pass near the
pheasant pens which will come very handy next summer. It's
such a perspective shift to get off the usual paths and still be in
exactly the same place, but have it be so different.

> *"The world is full of magic things, patiently waiting for our
> senses to grow sharper."*
> —W.B. Yeats

One of the most exciting things to open up seems to be connected to the Iron Age ancestor people who favoured this spot
to build forts, and standing stones, and stone cairns for their
dead. The look out position over the loch where I often sit had
it hidden in plain sight until somehow I passed the test, and
like a fairy door in the old stories, I was able to see it right before me. From the top of the hill down to the shore there is

a carved out path or avenue. It is lined with more stones that look both deliberate and carved to mark a passage. At first you think that must just be the natural landscape surely? But as you venture down the stones are placed vertically and even a great boulder appears to have been cut to make the way. 5000 years ago the bay would not have gone as far inwards and it makes sense that where this path pops out on the shore could very well have been the landing spot for approach by sea. I obviously have no evidence for this, just the dreaming between me and the land while I try to imagine what these people were doing in the same spot as me so very long ago.

I think I have found at least two more burial cairns as well. These are not in the same preserved shape as the two chambered cairn up by the house, but the same oyster shell carved shaped top stone lies near by and they are all in lovely spots about the landscape. It seems weird that

The two-chambered cairn.

there would only be one in what was so obviously an important spot. I need to find someone to write to who knows the area and ask if they would come and look at these unmarked spots. This part of Argyll is crawling with the deep history of the early peoples of the British Isles. Kilmartin Glen which is just a short drive from the cottage is the largest collection of Neolithic and Bronze Age remains in the country with over 800 ancient monuments within a six mile radius of the village. It will be interesting to learn more, or just keep imagining the people who were here so long ago.

In the Glasshouse

As you can imagine so much of the action at this time of year is happening in the greenhouse. And it's really been my sanctuary.

I've gotten many of my seeds in for the upcoming season including three varieties of tomatoes, peas, onions, kale, cucumbers, more sweet peas than I should have, some

Apricot blossoms.

ranunculus which I have been wishing to have for ages, and even some tulips and anemones outside in one of the abandoned planters by the house to see if we can make a go of it there. I was told it was the best antidote to winter dread, planting seeds for hope of abundance later in the year, so I've been busy!

But the big news has been the blossoming of the peach and apricot trees! I cannot wait until they are fully open and I have a little pink sanctuary for a few weeks.

The elder cuttings are growing well and I had such a burst of joy when my rhubarb plant decided that it would come back for the second year! Which means I will have my own fresh rhubarb this year if all goes well. What an investment gardening is! Nurturing something for sometimes years before ever expecting to get something out of it. If you would have told me a couple of years ago that I could make that commitment I would have been surprised. Now I dream of ten years to cultivate fruit and nut trees. But that will have to wait until I have my own place.

The calla lilies are thriving. The potatoes are chitting. The seeds are sprouting. (First up was a pea!) So all is well even with the dour weather. I even bought a second set of worms for the wormery this month, after the last bunch disappeared or disintegrated, and they seem to be thriving and happily attacking all the kitchen waste, so hopefully soon there will be some beautiful compost and fertiliser coming from there too. I expect

The elder cutting.

March will just be trying to keep up with what nature has in store for spring. I even get to build a raised garden outside the glasshouse doors this year so hopefully I'll be able to put some of the hardier plants out there and have a bit more of my own food grown here.

Nothing like Visitors

This month I also welcomed my youngest patron Sienna (6) and her mom for a four day stay over the school term break. Sienna and her brother Lincoln (who was away with his Dad so hasn't visited in person yet) have been subscribers from the very start of the letters. It was so wonderful to have her and her mum here. We did art together, we went looking for treasure on the beaches, we hid from the rain, took a ferry to go buy some fresh scallops and langoustine for dinner that night, chatted and generally had the best time. I also learned a lot of the words to the music from the new Annie movie—and maybe a couple of dance moves, but I wasn't very good at that part!

Sienna's mom Susan took some beautiful pictures of the

Loch Fyne scallops on my beautiful Atholl china.

food we were eating that showed off my china so well (all the images in this section) and of the quick friendship that happened between Sienna and Alfred. I love to see little humans and big dogs totally getting each other. It was such a great visit and I can't wait to welcome more of you here in 2020. The greatest pleasure remains writing to you each month and finding that you want to share this little adventure with me. Thank you for being here, and I'll be back in your mailbox next month.

Much love,
Susie
xx

Sienna and Alfred shot by her Mom.

MARCH 2020

The Gardeners Cottage
Argyll's Secret Coast
Scotland, UK

March 19, 2020

Oh my. Such a month since I last wrote to you. Unprecedented change and pause. Isn't it a bit amazing to witness how much caring for each other and ourselves has

There are at least six different daffodil species around the estate and that's why they get pride of place on your envelope this month!

NOT been built into the every day lives of our global cultures?

When I made this choice to come here to the Cottage, to learn to rest, to get back into an intimate relationship with the landscape and my own self, I already had a lot of questions about the value of what we call work and how we've pushed productivity far beyond its necessary bounds. I hope the "turn it off and reboot" we are going through helps us get better. I hope it doesn't cost us many more precious people while we learn how to take care of each other again.

Things here at the cottage are very calm. I can roam for miles without running into anyone. And my new neighbours turn out to contain a doctor! But I imagine if things get as serious as we expect he'll be quarantined at work so I hope to be of help to his young family. Living remotely I don't go to the store that often so I haven't been yet this month to measure if people out here have also lost their minds with hoarding. But our little local stores have had lots each time I'm in there so all is fine. There are things I don't know. I've had consulting work I was counting on delayed. I don't know whether or not my flat will sell now and I will be able to pay my bills through the means I had expected to. But I am sooooo fortunate and safe compared to so many. Your support each month has meant the world and once all the stamps and paper etc is bought each month there's a bill paid and a trip to the grocery store on you and I couldn't be more grateful.

Spring Equinox

Today is the Spring Equinox. The moment when the balance shifts to the light. That feels like very good news at the moment. We are at just over 12 hours of daylight again now and I am so delighted. Longer days are such a balm to my heart. I love that there is room for more outside time and still time to come in and cook and work at the computer and not feel like I was wasting it!

And although there hasn't been one glorious day where it suddenly felt like Spring was permanently here, the plants and trees and little creatures have all been so reliable reminding me that it was still coming. In the last few days it has started to tip the balance with more blooms poking their heads up and the first butterfly spotting of the year.

There are a thousand or more daffodils in bloom now around the cottage and the other houses on the estate. There are at least six different kinds. And slowly the showy things are starting to raise their heads. The glowing pink of the magnolia tree at the top of the hill, the heather along the burn, the camellia trees, and the other outdoor fruit trees on the edge of blossoming.

These beautiful snails are called Topshells because of their decorate mother of pearl tops like vessels from the east. They are important grazers of micro-algae and things along the shore keeping it clean.

My adventures down the deer trails to parts previously unexplored continues. I've found so many treasured spots. Perfect picnic hideaways. Abandoned stone walls and ancient trees so wrapped in moss you can't reach the bark. Am I the only one who always touches them to feel the springy-ness? There is something incredibly special about exploring warn pathways created by other animals. To literally step into their ordinary day and travels like riding public transport in a foreign city. You imagine yourself a bit more local to their experience. And although the ticks will soon awaken with all the other creatures I am treasuring this time of deepening my relationship to the landscape and quieter or more secluded inhabitants of the estate.

My long-awaited visit from my friend who is a conservation expert has coincided with the beginning of the coronavirus outbreak. She's here now, and may be for a lot longer than she originally planned! But we've been enjoying ourselves so much—between news broadcasts— retracing so many of my own steps and seeing the abundance of the landscape here through her eyes.

One of the most exciting things I've learned is that my wonderful little peninsula that I visit most days is a long established and regularly frequented otter territory! There is otter poo and trails everywhere!!! And what I also learned was that Alfred may have known about them for

Otter teeth marks on its snack of a small crab left alongside the loch.

some time before I did, because we have walked those trails before along the edge of the rocks and he basically goes from mound to mound eating their poo!!! So that's a new talent of his we've discovered!

It will be absolutely sensational to spot them now that I know to look. Isn't that an amazing thing to learn? I was sharing paths with them everyday without the information to know that they were there. Now that I know, I can never not see the signs of them everywhere! They love crabs, sea urchins, and mus-

This beautiful creature is called a Sea Hare. I found it one morning in the shallows of the tide.

sels and leave distinctive little tooth marks on the shells. Hopefully I'll be able to report a sighting to you in the future. Fran, as an Otters and Rivers Officer previously in Sussex, hadn't seen that much evidence of them in years and was so thrilled. Even more reason to protect our wild spaces and help the tame spaces rewild in ways that we can too.

In the Glasshouse and Foraging

Things in the glasshouse and gardening portion of life here are going so very well. As news of the food hoarding was hitting I did take a little stock and realise that I had planted 3-1 more flowers than food! So I've done some more basics sowing in the last couple of weeks of things like lettuce and radishes that will be available early. But honestly there is so much to learn about foraging around these parts that I'm excited to see how I can get even better at supplementing and substituting local, wild growing things for flavouring and nutrition. We had nettle, wild garlic, and new season chives in a lovely vegetable soup for lunch today. It was wonderful!

Mussels foraged for dinner.

My hope is to be able to ferment some wild garlic for sharing. I've got chives drying and I recently found a lovely supply of Pepper Dulse. It's a small brown seaweed that you have to find at really low tide. Pepper pulse is called the truffle of the sea. You can cut it straight from the rock and have a taste and you'll be so thrilled with the earthy truffle hint and then still the  umami quality of the seaweed. I'm drying some for flavouring as truffled mashed potatoes and French fries are basically one of my favourite things on the planet! Did you know that in the UK any seaweed that is growing and you can reach on foot is edible? They aren't all the tastiest apparently, but none of them are poisonous. And in fact it is said the the seaweed Dulse is what the Vikings survived on through their long sea voyages! We've forgotten so many things. And I love learning each new thing I can, and sharing it onwards, to keep our collective memory vibrant!

If you are interested in foraging there are so many lovely sources on the internet. I started just by following some people on Instagram. Then took a day course. Keep buying books and getting more brave while being 100% sure of each thing before I try it. I'd love to hear about forgotten foods around your homes if you find them!

In the glasshouse my little sweet pepper has revived on its own. This year I also am trying to start some lavender and jalapeño peppers! I'll let you know how I get on. It's all such an experiment for me. I have been allowed to build a small raised bed across from the glasshouse too this year, so hopefully I can move some of the bigger things (that deer don't like to eat!) into that space. I just need to buy the compost for it now and wait for the outdoor planting weather.

I'll leave you this month with these lovely words form the glorious Irish poet John O'Donohue. I wish you health, comfort, and all the good that a deep pause might be bringing us.

"This is the time to be slow, Lie low to the wall
Until the bitter weather passes.
Try, as best you can, not to let The wire brush of doubt Scrape
from your heart
All the sense of yourself And your hesitant light.
If you remain generous, Time will come good;
And you will find your feet Again on fresh pastures of promise, Where
the air will be kind
And blushed with beginning."
—John O'Donohue

Much love,
Susie
xx

APRIL 2020

The Gardeners Cottage
Argyll's Secret Coast
Scotland, UK

April 21, 2020

My dear friends. How com-
pletely strange the times are.
One minute I have nothing
but joy and peace to report to you, the next I am full of sorrow
and exhaustion and not
even sure how to start. I don't imagine I am alone in this wild
vacillation of feeling and energy at the moment. My daily life
is relatively unchanged, but amidst the peace of it all I've found
myself quite unsettled. It's really only when I'm sat outside
somewhere sprawled beside the loch with a cup of tea or deep
under the trees that I feel really calm. The rest of the time I've
felt this compulsion to be very busy—without really accom-
plishing anything of note—so I find myself even more tired,
and yet needing to drag myself back out into nature to calm
down. It's strange and unsettling and I'm not quite at the point
where I quite understand what's happening inside myself yet.
Obviously, times like this bring up all sorts of things for attention and perhaps even healing.

I keep finding passageways in the landscape this month.
Like the one above. I feel like that's one of the messages for us
now. To pass through. For us to emerge from this crisis with
more appreciation of the impact of our human world (as it is
currently constructed) on nature, on the most vulnerable people, on the most average people with our compulsion to pro-
duce and measure success only by measuring for "more" and

busy-ness. I want us to see more clearly that making some people disposable has been part of our ordinary for quite a while, and I dream that we make ourselves heard by how much we disagree with it now that more of us have seen it so clearly and close to home. I feel some days like I'm sitting vigil next to nature waiting for the turn of the tides amongst us.

This morning I sat just above the rising water and wondered how at this important moment it could possibly be my role to BE here, be peaceful, to observe and share the nature around me? How could that be right and valuable? I was so trained to DO. To find all my value in the doing. I always wanted to do something important. I was always worried about doing good things, but now I wonder what would be different if I focused on being good? And here at the cross-roads of our time I find mine, and a lot of our roles, to prioritise figuring out how to be, be better, be more ourselves, be more connected, be more kind in thought and deed. Be. So here I am in this spot at this time, taking my cues from nature and deeply surrendering to my position and sharing the experience.

And because my "self" also loves to laugh, I remembered this funny sign (right) I used to have in my office for 15 years. I was preparing for this from long ago! Do be do be do loves!

I've been disappointed to have to delay so many wonderful visitors that were to be here with me from next month and getting to experience the joys of the cottage and the grounds for themselves. I love sharing it and it's an adjustment to know I won't be able to in person for a while. I've redoubled my efforts to share a bit of the nature and beauty around me here on social media for everyone who might be stranded far from it.

A Message in a Bottle

At the end of last month my guest Fran came home from a walk with a message in a bottle she had discovered on one of the more remote beaches while she was off looking for otters. What a delightful thing to happen! It took us a few attempts to get the paper out to realise we were going to have to break in to get it. So I put it in a cloth bag and smashed it against  the picnic table and revealed this lovely treat.

Here's the transcript as written:

8 July 2017

Hello there!

I'm Henrique from Portugal. I'm sending this from Mull of Kintyre Island, Scotland. I'm travelling threw Scotland on a boat, and it's been delightful! Anyway I was wondering if you have ever eaten a Bifana? It's like a Portugues version of a tasty pork sandwich with garlic. YUMMY! So

Please answer me by sending me an email telling me if you did infact eaten a bifana or not. If you haven't you really should. Well goodbye, and best of days for you! May Scotland and Portugal be the best of friends forever!

Also I would like to add that bifana goes lovely with haggis. And if for any reason your not from Scotland, please do send me an answer anyway!

I wrote back to Henrique at the enclosed email address, telling him that I had not had a Bifana and showing him where we picked up the message.

This was the return message:

Hello!! So very nice to receive this message!!

I was just completely mind blown by your mail! It's been so long since I thrown that out of the boat to the wild and beautiful sea of Scotland. I never thought someone would actually receive it, because I left it in place with only desert islands surrounding it and seals wandering around ahah. I can't recall where it was I left it, but I'm going to ask the boat owner, he'll probably remember a lot more. So thought full of you to send me the location thanks a lot!

Ahahah, yes you should try the famous Bifana, you won't regret it. Simple but tasty.

Could you send me a picture of the message in the bottle? I can't fully remember what was on it and I'm sure it will be very funny to read it. Such a lovely place Scotland.

It is still to this day one of my most, if not the most, enjoyable vacation, and I am sure to return.

Here in Lisbon we are in quarantine, as I suppose you are, but we are hanging in strong, and soon things will be back to normal. May everything go for the best for you, and for Scotland! Thank you for replying for my long awaited message!

With best regards,
Henrique, Cascais, Lisbon.

What a wonderful thing to happen across time and space. A wish for friendship dropped off a boat into the sea. Three years floating, then marooned only to emerge in time for a message between quarantined societies to re-express all the good wishes and warm thoughts of each other's experience and place in the world. A bit magic I wanted to share with you all!

In the Greenhouse

In this extraordinary sunny weather we are experiencing right now there is no warmer place than the greenhouse to sit—it borders on tropical all afternoon with its full sun and protection from the wind. I sat here in the afternoon painting all your envelopes and now I'm sitting here writing to you. The rest of the house with its 2 foot walls is chilled and it seems a shame to run the heat when I can be out here in the sunshine surrounded by buzzing bees.

The plant action in here is very busy! It such a thrilling time of year to have a greenhouse. My efforts with the feather and the apricot blossoms seem to have paid off. The tree is in full leaf already and some of the fruit is shockingly large. I don't know if the crop will be as generous as last year, but there will be a crop and I am delighted.

Pear blossoming in the walled garden.

I do predict a bumper year for peaches though. Last year the peaches were a bit choked by the jasmine, clematis, and even the grape vine and the apricot tree overshadowed them. There were about six peaches in total that made it to full growth and even those didn't taste very special. The effort to free them up some space has seemed to pay off in spades and there are hundreds of small fruit growing between the two trees. I'll do some reading to see whether or not I'm to thin them out a bit, but watch this space for homemade peach gelato hopefully!!

The two calla lilies have come back to their stunning full proportions. As I write you there are at least 19 blooms, all about 3 feet high and looking like my own private, graceful collection of Georgia O'Keeffe paintings.

In the pots and trays I've tried to get a much earlier start on vegetable things. The lettuce and radish that I planted last month are days away from being ready to harvest. The first tomatoes have gone onto the big pots and are staked and ready for their best efforts. I've got about 20 tomatoes in general going at the moment! I have promised to trade them with my neighbour for her potato efforts outside. This year I'm trying kale, onions, beets, cabbage, cucumbers, courgette, peas, strawberries, and hopefully some peppers. I have been assigned a dire little plot outside who needs about a year's work really before it can be useful. But I've started some sunflowers, corn, and lovely wildflowers (thank you Caroline) to try and reclaim the edges to start. I've got it covered with some discarded carpet fragments at the moment to help kill off the weeds until the little plants are ready to go out. It will be a good experiment!

On the flower side the many sweet peas are doing well. I'm trying to work out a little potting and climbing structure for them out of a washed up lobster or crab pot from the beach and a driftwood and fishing rope ladder. I'll show you what I manage if it's successful. The lavender seed has sprouted, but I'm not sure I'm winning that just yet. It's funny how some things grow perfectly for you and others aren't as pleased with the conditions.

In the walled garden all the pear trees are in bloom and as the daffodils and primrose begin to fade I am watching for signs of the iris that was such a wonderful surprise last year.

April has belonged to the birds mostly. Long absent friends are spotted and heard again. I've heard the first cuckoo, the woodpeckers are busy, busy. The tawny owl males who call around here most nights have even had a responding female "twit" for their "twoos." And they've been joined by the horror movie screech of the barn owl many nights—not quite as poetic! I spend my days looking up bird species in my lovely books and on the internet trying to figure out who everyone is. There are Greylag and Canada Geese, Shelduck and Mallards.

My favourite have been the very funny ducks on the loch called Eider Ducks - a UK Amber Level Conservation species. They are true sea ducks and are the UK's heaviest and fastest flying. The males are black and white, females are brown. The males follow the females around throwing back their heads,

155. EIDER, *Somateria mollissima* ♀ ♂

The Eider Duck a historical illustration.
Birds in Colour, Karl Aage Tinggaard

puffing up, and making a sound like ah-wooo wooo. I love watching them and wish I could send you a video. But here's a lovely illustration of them from my "Birds in Colour" book to show you how handsome they are so you can imagine them.

With all my time spent by the shore the seals have also been putting on some fine shows! They are so curious. During one of the very low spring tides I was almost able to reach their islands (Eilean Buide —yellow islands in Gaelic).

The creature on the envelope this month is the Red Squirrel. We are so lucky to have them in Scotland and here on the estate I call one part of the road Red Squirrel alley. These cheeky little fellows are in precipitous decline in the UK, the larger grey squirrels which are an invasive species totally out match them and drove them out of traditional territories all. But interesting things are happening as the Pine Martin species recovers. The Grey Squirrels don't have the same instincts to not be captured by them as they did not evolve near them, where the red squirrel was in an eco-system with them for thousands of years! So where the martins are doing well, so are the red squirrels! I hope he cheered your day when he arrived.

All the Pretty Flowers

The wild flowers are also having their time. Smaller in stature than what's happening in the cultivated gardens, their little faces pushing through the dead bracken or at the foot of a tree do make me so very happy though. And surely that's the point?

Isn't that the only way to curate a life? To live among things that make you gasp with delight?

-Maira Kalman

Breaking News!!!

I had left your letter, thinking I was finished at the quote, but I kept hearing the scene from the end of the ABBA Movie during the credits where Meryl Streep in full costume joyfully, obviously having more fun than anyone, asks. "Do you want a little more???" So I went for a walk and low and behold I have more. And I figure as everyone is social distancing we deserve an extra page this month!

I wanted to write about how my intimacy with the land has exponentially increased this year. All the new nooks and crannies. Some I've written about already. The way more and more areas and secrets are being revealed to me. Beckoning of new paths and further views. Hidden, moss covered rock faces and little birch forests clear of bracken. Yesterday I found another ancient oak tree in a hidden little glen between the path and the steep shore line. It is so huge and solid. One of the branches alone is so big that I wouldn't be about to half wrap my arms around it. For an oak growing up in these challenging weather conditions in Scotland that indicates really great age. (Greater than 300 years but most likely in the four hundred range. Can you even imagine that???)

So the breaking news, while I was leaving your letter to cool for a final edit, on my walk I FOUND ANOTHER STANDING STONE!!!! This brings the count, that I know of, on the estate to four. I saw it today just a couple of hundred feet from where I often am. An approach of a hill from a slightly different direction and the sun shining in just the right way through the naked trees and there it was. Under the canopy of a lovely old beech and amongst some other broken tree stumps to camouflage. It is isolated on a little promontory between the stream and a fence. It took me a bit to figure out how to get across the steep banks of the stream to get to it. But I did. It's as tall as I am and a soft brown slate colour. What a thing to appear to me today.

I think there is so much we aren't seeing right in front of us, like this stone.

My wish for you this month is that you also have an experience of new eyes and exploration in the intimate landscape around you—even if its just your windowsill.

Stay well and we'll speak again soon.

Much love,
Susie xx

THE ART OF AN ENVELOPE

Even before moving to The Gardeners Cottage I had always loved to draw on my envelopes. Why should the pleasure of receiving a letter only start when you open it? There were birthday cards with cakes and balloons drawing the attention of whoever delivered the post to a celebration. Or a silly sketch of my Old English Sheepdog Alfred would hope to make people smile. So when I conceived the letters subscription I of course thought to include it as a feature. Little did I know that the practise of repetitively painting a creature or scene would become another pillar of rewilding myself right along with the ability to notice nature around me. The release of perfection and sameness that comes from repeating an image--in the early days 10 times and more recently seventy plus times!--has been a particular kind of unbinding. It gives me great satisfaction and has made me so incredibly tolerant of myself as a creator in a way that, despite my abilities when a child and in university, I never possessed. I highly recommend it!

May: The Great Tit

June: Foxglove

July: Common Seals

August: Peacock Butterfly

September: The constellation Aquila

October: Heron

November: A Coo Stampede

December: Christmas Thistles

January: Sheep

February: Windswept Trees

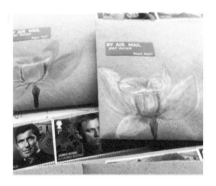

March: Daffodils

April: Red Squirrel

How to Get A Letter

If you'd like to subscribe to receive or gift your own copies
of Letters from The Gardeners Cottage
visit me on Patreon at
www.patreon.com/thegardenerscottage.